The Windows of Heaven

The Windows of Heaven

IRENE HARRELL

Word Books, Publisher
Waco, Texas

First Printing, November 1975
Second Printing, April 1976

WINDOWS OF HEAVEN

ISBN 0-87680-994-8

Library of Congress catalog card number: 75–19902
Printed in the United States of America.

to

the glory of God

Father

Son

and Holy Spirit

and to the Rock Church

Wilson, NC,

in whose fellowship

we have experienced

the fullness

of the Body of Christ

Contents

Preface

This is the day the Lord has made. And it seems the right day to begin putting together a third book of *Prayerables*.

How much God has taught me since the first one began! Even the second one seems light years in the past. And yet the truths he revealed to me then are still truths because his truths are eternal and infinite, capable of being understood on many levels, depending on what depth of understanding we bring to them.

Back in those days, my favorite Scripture—perhaps because it was about the only one I knew—was Romans 8:28, how all things work together for good to those who love God, who are called according to his purpose.

But he's been doing a new thing in our lives and in the world. And "things working together for good" is far too feeble a phrase to describe the exuberance I have known lately about the way God is moving. Currently, the verse I want to proclaim and share everywhere is the one found in Malachi 3:10. (As I read it, I don't interpret in a limited legalistic way the word *tithe*, but I understand it to mean all that God's entitled to, which is everything I am and have.)

> Bring ye all the tithes into the storehouse, that there may be meat in mine house, and prove me now herewith, saith the Lord of hosts, if I will not open you the windows of heaven, and pour you out a blessing, that there shall not be room enough to receive it.

And how he does it! No matter what the circumstance,

how dark the clouds, when I choose to give him everything and to praise him for it, he keeps on opening the windows of heaven. Truly, there is not room in my heart or in all the world to contain the joy and the thanksgiving that he brings to me.

My prayer is that this book will be God's instrument to bring to you an increased awareness of who he is and what he is even now doing for you.

Lord, let these pages be veritable windows of heaven, through which you may pour blessings abundant upon the children you love.

1

My Father Made It

A long crate arrived at our house a few weeks ago. In it was a grandfather clock that my father had just made for us. How we loved it. How wonderful it was to hear the Westminster chimes every quarter hour and be reminded of him and the hours of loving craftsmanship that he poured out to make such a clock for each of his six children. How we treasured it.

Every visitor at our house has been taken into the living room to admire its satiny walnut elegance. If the visitor couldn't stay long enough to hear the clock chime in the normal course of things, we'd move the hands forward, so he or she could enjoy the sound of the chimes at least once.

"My father made it," I told everybody proudly.

This morning, our teenage Susan was coming through the hallway upstairs right after the sun had come up. It was shining through the window of my bedroom, and the door was open.

"Oh, just look at the gorgeous sun!" she exclaimed.

"My Father made it," I said to her, and we both laughed, sharing the joyful preciousness of the moment.

This afternoon, Allen and I went to the hospital to visit a man in the intensive care unit. He was critically ill, and we had both been overwhelmed with the love of Jesus as we prayed for him. When we came out of the hospital, the sky was ablaze with sunset, and the intricate branchings of bare trees silhouetted against it took my breath away.

"My Father made it *for me*," I heard myself say.

O Lord, how marvelous your love toward us from our birth until our going home. How unbelievably beautiful your creation, from the rising of the sun to the going down of it. Thank you for showing us that our Father made it—for us—and give us to remember, whenever we see a tree, a flower, the ocean, a rock, a blade of grass —anything of beauty in all of creation—that the Lord God made it all, and that you made it just for us because you love. Thank you, Lord.

The mighty God, even the Lord, hath spoken, and called the earth from the rising of the sun unto the going down thereof. Out of Zion, the perfection of beauty, God hath shined (Ps. 50:1–2).

2

Happy Motherhood

How to be a happier mother? There are lots of recipes
for that, but one worth remembering is to train yourself
to see
>   a fragile lace medallion
>   in the dirty suds circles
>   left on the fresh cake of soap
>   by an in-to-eat toddler
>   from the sandpile.

*O Lord, I have fretted so much in my lifetime about
the messes kids make. Just yesterday, I blew up at the
little ones who had sneaked outside and gotten absolutely
mired down in the mud of the garden—looking for a
turnip, I think they said. They lost a half-pair of shoes
and a pair and a half of almost new mittens, to say nothing of getting soaked to the skin when I thought I had
finished the laundry for one day. How I fretted.*

*And then you showed me what life must be like for
some of the rich ladies in fine homes who have no little
ones to bring in mud—or laughter—untold interruptions
worth a day. Lord, forgive me that I'm so often griping
about the very things that give my life meaning.*

*How I'll miss my muddy little urchins when they're
grown and gone. Lord, is that why grandparents enjoy*

their grandchildren so much—being aware of how soon the child's days are past and life is serious business forevermore? Lord, I look forward to my grandchildren, but let me enjoy my children now, to the fullest.

And thank you, Lord, that you've given me the very best, the most wonderful life imaginable by giving me children.

Lo, children are an heritage of the Lord (Ps. 127:3).

3

Come, Heavenly Dove

As we turned into the driveway of the little church, I saw a dove light on the lawn to the left of the car. It remained there for a moment, apparently unaware of our presence, as if it wanted to stay, as if it didn't want to have to fly away. Lingering a little, was she saying, "Here am I forever"? But no, it was not to be. We watched her as she whirred away. If she ever came back, I haven't heard about it.

Lord, if that tiny whispering symbol of your Holy Spirit had abode there, as it did on Jesus, I wonder what a church that would be today. Lord, help all the churches that claim your precious name, to let you abide. Let them let you be in charge even of the order of worship on Sunday mornings instead of forever kowtowing to the paper and ink excrement of some mimeograph machine that works only on Wednesdays. And Lord, make me able to turn the order of my life entirely to you also. Sometimes I wish you'd make us partake of the freedom your Spirit brings.

Now this Lord is the Spirit, and where the Spirit of the Lord is, there is freedom (2 Cor. 3:17, JB).

15

4

The Hairs of Your Head

The woman was telling me how it happened, an incident that I hadn't seen myself but had heard about afterward.

"I saw the comb lying under his chair," she said. "And naturally I picked it up and tapped him on the shoulder and asked him, 'Is this your comb?'"

"No, that's not mine," he said.

"Well, it was right under your chair," she had said, rather insistently.

"Well, what would I use it for?" he asked her, seeming almost annoyed that she persisted.

"Well, everybody uses a comb," she said.

"Well, it's not mine." He walked away. As she looked after his retreating figure, her jaw dropped. She stood there devastated, the comb still in her outstretched hand.

She hadn't yet recovered when she told me, "I never realized—he was the baldest man I'd ever seen. There wasn't a single wisp of hair, not a scrap of fuzz, anywhere on his head. I had sat behind him the whole time and never noticed until he walked away."

Lord, I know how she must have felt. I'm that unseeing, that unnoticing, so much of the time. Once in a while I find it out when someone brings me up short about it

17

—generally your Holy Spirit. Someone can come to our house with a great burden on his heart, and I keep talking so much, telling all that's going on in our lives and seldom inquiring about theirs, that sometimes they leave, never even having had a chance to mention something of vast importance, because I am so self-centered.

I think of one friend in particular, Lord. Why, every time she walks in the door, I begin to pour out every detail of all my concerns. And later, maybe, I learn what a heavy burden her heart bore that day, and I'm so ashamed I want to go and hide somewhere. Lord, please, please, make me more mindful of the needs of others. Let me listen for the heart-cries of others before I sound off about my own.

Are not two sparrows sold for a farthing? and one of them shall not fall on the ground without your Father knowing. But the very hairs of your head are all numbered. Fear ye not therefore, ye are of more value than many sparrows (Matt. 10:29–31).

5

Mechanical Mystery

I can't remember how old Alice was, the day she went to spend part of the day in the law office with her daddy. Nor do I recall how long she stayed or what the occasion was that required him to practice law with a little tyke in tow. But it was a day that impressed her, all right. I remember asking her about it when she came home. She allowed that she'd had a good enough time—she'd liked it, she said, looking still strangely awed by it all.

"What did you do?" I asked her, trying to draw out some more details. She probably told me that she had colored, or drawn some pictures, or played with the paperclips in her daddy's desk. Finally, after a significant pause, she asked, "Mama, what was that man doing? Why was he winding that little grinder thing?"

I was as mystified as she was until further questioning of her and her daddy elicited the information that the man with whom he shared a suite of offices, and a superexcellent secretary, had come into Allen's office a time or two to sharpen his pencil.

Lord, there are a lot of things in life that mystify me, too. I might puzzle profoundly over something as simple to you as winding that little grinder thing would have been to Alice a few years later after she turned into a pencil-sharpening schoolgirl herself. I praise you, Lord, for all the things that you will unfold to me in the fullness of your time when I am old enough to know and understand.

I have yet many things to say unto you, but ye cannot bear them now. Howbeit when he, the Spirit of truth, is come, he will guide you into all truth (John 16:12–13).

A Gray Day

We were vacationing at Emerald Isle on June 14, 1973.
It wasn't a sunny day altogether, and I saw
    rain erasing
      the horizon
        making sea and sky
          the same
    blending heaven and earth.

*Lord, I like it when you do that spiritually, too, when
you bring heaven so near that there seems no difference
between earth and heaven because heaven could be no
more joyful than you have given us to be in the here
and now. I wish I had already become the kind of person
who could receive that gift from you more often. But
maybe it's better this way, that we grow gradually into
what would be too much for us to bear if we arrived all
at once.*

We confidently and joyfully look forward to actually
becoming all that God has had in mind for us to be
(Rom. 5:2, LB).

Thorns and Thistles

"You know, I've decided that thorns are of the devil," Jamie, our host, said, picking up a long piece of briar that lay across the woodspath where four of us were walking one July afternoon. "I've spent some time out here clearing up, and the things actually seem to reach out and grab you, like they're evil and alive, deliberately malicious."

"Really?" I asked. "Don't you think there is anything good about them?" He shook his head. "But," I protested, "when God made everything, he saw that it was good. I don't like to think of any of his creation as being evil—" I reminded him that we'd noticed that thorns grow in starlike patterns around the stems of rose and blackberry briars. And stars led wise men to worship Jesus.

"I don't know about that," Jamie said. "I just know these thorns seem to me to be intrinsically evil."

We dropped the discussion then, but I kept on thinking about what he had said and wondering about it. Why *did* God make thorns and briars? And all the other things like thistles and houseflies and mosquitoes that we find so unpleasant to live with? He must have had a good reason.

The next morning, I sat down in a high-backed rocking

chair on the porch overlooking the majestic mountains that rose so mysteriously all around us. I had my Bible in my lap and knew that my question—as any question—would be answered somewhere in its pages. Somehow I was not led to open it at random to receive the answer to this one, but to begin at the beginning, to look at the account of creation and see what God would reveal to me.

Beginning at Genesis 1:1, I was blessed, as I read, to be reminded of how God made the day and the night, the dry land and seas, fish and birds and fruit and animals—and all the rest of it. Then there was man, and woman, and her confrontation with the serpent. When God spoke to the serpent and to Adam and Eve after their transgression in eating the forbidden fruit, he told them what their punishment would be.

"And to Adam, God said, 'Because you listened to your wife and ate the fruit when I told you not to, I have placed a curse upon the soil. All your life you will struggle to extract a living from it. It will grow thorns and thistles for you . . .'" (Gen. 3:17–18, LB).

Oh! God didn't create thorns in the beginning, but only after man sinned.

Thank you, Lord, that no distress in the world is of your original and perfect will but is occasioned by our disobedience to the good life you have planned for us in your infinite wisdom. Make us learn that when we all come to rest in your will for our lives, we will not have the frustrations and vexations, the thorns and briars of life, but we will inherit the kingdom you have prepared for us from the beginning of the world. And thank you for your promise that in that kingdom where lions and lambs lie down together, "Nothing will hurt or destroy in all my holy mountain" (Isa. 11:9, LB).

O Lord, make us obedient so that your perfect kingdom can be manifested among us. Thank you, Lord. AMEN.

If my people, which are called by my name, shall humble themselves, and pray, and seek my face, and turn from their wicked ways; then will I hear from heaven, and will forgive their sin, and will heal their land (2 Chron. 7:14).

Domestic Difficulty

Oh, the problems they'd had in their marriage—and continued to have. It was inevitable, what with their marrying and having a baby when she was only thirteen and he in his thirties already—that and his heavy drinking that turned him into a brute who beat the children and abused her every weekend so that she dreaded to see the days roll by. She was pouring it all out to us for the umpteenth time, telling how he would come in at three or four o'clock in the morning. When she'd ask where he'd been, he'd say, "I've been with a woman who wants me."

O Lord, how we all need to be wanted, how we want to be needed. Please, Lord, in our family, let us all acknowledge that we need one another, that we want one another. Let love keep cementing us together, especially love of you.

A man shall leave his father and his mother, and shall cleave to his wife; and they shall become one flesh (Gen. 2:24, NAS).

To the woman he said, . . . Your desire shall be for your husband, And he shall rule over you (Gen. 3:16, NAS).

9

Just Plain, Nothing Fancy

When we took Maria to the circus for the first time, she was too open-mouthed with awe at all that was going on around her to say much. But in the weeks that followed, I learned what had impressed her most, by things she said or asked about. I had been aware at the time that she had paid close attention to a boy who had come to see the circus. He wasn't in a wheelchair, but something was wrong with his legs—they were twisted backward, or halfway paralyzed—and he had struggled in with two girls—his sisters, maybe?—helping to support him down the aisle.

About the same time, Maria had become acquainted with a young girl who had been born without a thumb on her left hand.

One afternoon she seemed unusually thoughtful, and I knew that something was coming. Finally she said, "Mama, that boy at the circus was born with his legs on wrong, and Ellen was born with her thumb all gone, but I was born just plain, wasn't I?"

She sounded like she felt cheated, somehow, being born "just plain," with nothing remarkable about her.

O Lord, I'm so thankful for your mercy to Maria. That although she was born with something gravely wrong

with her—the doctors had diagnosed her as at least se-
verely hard of hearing and maybe profoundly deaf—you
heard every prayer prayed for her and healed her so com-
pletely that she hears everything and has no remembrance
of ever being anything except perfectly "plain." I praise
you, Lord. And I pray for the boy with twisted legs, and
for the girl who lacks a thumb, and lift them up to you,
that they may experience your healing wholeness in their
lives too. In Jesus' name.

Jesus now returned to the Sea of Galilee, and climbed
a hill and sat there. And a vast crowd brought him
their lame, blind, maimed, and those who couldn't
speak, and many others, and laid them before Jesus,
and he healed them all. What a spectacle it was!
Those who hadn't been able to say a word before
were talking excitedly, and those with missing
arms and legs had new ones; the crippled were walking and jumping around, and those who had been
blind were gazing about them! The crowds just mar-
veled, and praised the God of Israel (Matt. 15:29–
31, LB).

10

A Prayer about Interruptions

I found the prayer in an old notebook, a spiritual one I had kept for a while after I first came to know God. It didn't sound put-on; it sounded like I really meant it:

"O Lord, I thank thee that thou hast freed me from all interruptions for thy Son's sake. That though the phone may ring, the doorbell shrill when I have sat me down to write, these are never interruptions as long as I am conscious of being your servant, at work only for thee. Then each former interruption becomes instead a golden opportunity to love one for whom Christ died and so love that he and I will be closer drawn to thee. Can there be any greater gift than this? A life free of frustration and interruption, with everything that happens, even to appliances breaking down (because one of your children will fix it), in accord with thy purpose and because thine, mine also, for my life. Nothing extraneous then, because in thee I am perfectly set free.

"And now with unscheduled opportunities temporarily at an end I apply myself to the task set for me and ask that you would bless even it to the glory of thy name. Amen."

Lord, forgive me that I haven't felt that way lately, that indeed I'd almost forgotten that point of view, grit-

31

ting my teeth at even pleasant things that disrupted my schedule. Remind me anew, and keep me reminded, that I have no time that does not belong to you, and let me rejoice as you use it to please yourself and not me. Restore the prayer to me, and me to it, Lord, that you might bless me and let me be a blessing—yes, even me.

What? know ye not that your body is the temple of the Holy Ghost which is in you, which ye have of God, and ye are not your own? For ye are bought with a price (1 Cor. 6:19, 20).

Reflected Glory

Whitebreasted snowbird,
How are you knowing?
Wherever you're going
Tomorrow it's snowing.

Snowbirds were new to me when I married and moved south. I don't know whether we had them in Ohio or not. My bird knowledge there was so limited, I knew the difference between a blue jay and a cardinal and a robin, but not between a sparrow and a starling or a towhee and a thrasher. Anyway, I love to see the little juncos now, their snowy breasts reflecting the snow that's yet to come, when the ground is still brown with dry grass or fallen leaves.

Thank you, Lord for the instincts of your creatures, for all they seem to know, all we can learn from their behavior. And thank you, Lord, especially for snowbirds and what the ones in my yard have shown me today. Just as they reflect the glory of the snow before it comes, so we are to reflect your glory, the glory of your love, before your physical appearing among us. Let us grow in grace so that all who see us will know that you yourself are on the way, that you are coming soon.

And we, with our unveiled faces reflecting like mirrors the brightness of the Lord, all grow brighter and brighter as we are turned into the image that we reflect; this is the work of the Lord who is Spirit (2 Cor. 3:18, JB).

Vacation

There were little ripples leaping up out of the brownish green river water sloshing at the shore. I sat in a lawn chair in the front yard of someone else's cottage and just drank it in, enjoying, savoring everything about the day. Sure, the cottage needed paint; there were cobwebs in the windows. The painted metal chair in which I sat had rust spots on it that needed sanding down. But it was someone else's property, and I could enjoy the cobwebs, marveling at their symmetry, feeling no responsibility for chasing them away or disturbing the spider at his work.

Lord, I need to be able to be like that at home and not have to go off for a vacation. Lord, I thank you that your word tells me to labor six days and rest on the seventh so that there is some time when my conscience doesn't nag me to be up and doing but to be still and know that you are God, to enjoy the now *of that marvelous truth instead of saving it for some never-to-be all-caught-up tomorrow. Let the home you have given me be as a rented river cottage once in a while, the cobwebs, the dust, the finger-marked windows not even my business. Thank you, Lord, for times of rest in my soul.*

This is the rest wherewith ye may cause the weary to rest; and this is the refreshing (Isa. 28:12).

Maelstrom Below

It was in the midst of what had been a rather hectic holiday season. I couldn't call it a vacation for me, what with all six children home for the holidays, plus visiting roommates, fiancées, aunts, and boyfriends keeping our usual number at the dinner table ten or above. Early that morning, I was dimly aware that someone had gotten up, one of the little people, and was downstairs pushing a relatively quiet rolling toy across the kitchen floor. No need for me to attend to that just then, and it wasn't quite the deadline for me to get out of bed; so I rolled over for a little extra nap.

Just then our five-year-old went clomping down the stairs. She had on her teenage brother's boots, from the sound of it. Well, that was all right too; it could be ignored. But then the booted one began to shout at the truck-roller, " 'Guerite, you're making too much noise! Mama wants you to be quiet so she can sleep." Not having her hearing aid on yet for the day, 'Guerite failed to hear her or at least failed to heed her. The soft background noise of the rolling truck continued to sound below the more fiercely crescendoing every minute shouting of the little one. " 'Guerite, mama wants you to be quiet so she can sleep!"

Well, Lord, I got up. You know there was no use staying in bed after the meleé that began downstairs directly below me. The one trying to quiet the other was by far the most distracting influence for miles around. It was kind of funny and then I realized how like the five-year-old I am. Often. To correct some minor ill, I create a whole host of worse ones. Forgive me, Lord. Show me when I ought to leave well-enough alone, and make me obedient to it. Thank you, Lord.

So no matter who you are, if you pass judgment you have no excuse. In judging others you condemn yourself, since you behave no differently from those you judge (Rom. 2:1, JB).

14

On Backing Up
to Get a Running Start

When we were kids, it was not unusual for us to back up to get a running start in a race. Appropriate enough for kids, I think, but I keep on doing that when the wisdom of it is past. It seems I'm forever backing up to get a running start on overcoming some besetting sin in my life. Only I never win the race. I just keep getting further and further from the starting line—further behind it, not in front of it. For instance, when I'm aware that the pointer on the scales has reached never-never land, I resolve, firmly, of course, to cut down, to diet—tomorrow, after I've finished the box of chocolates on top of the refrigerator.

Lord, what makes me like that? Is there any hope I'll ever change? Give me, somehow, by your sovereign grace, to know that there may not be a tomorrow when I can do the things I have failed to do today. Let my every good resolve be a for-now, this-moment one, not putting off until tomorrow the remedying of a situation I should never have allowed to develop in the first place—

Oh, excuse me, Lord. There I go again, thinking I can remedy something, thinking the right kind of resolve in me can accomplish anything. Thank you, Lord, that I will forever fail, no matter where I start from.

Thank you, Lord, that I can't change myself but that you are abundantly able to make me a new creature again and again as I trust in you. Allow me to trust you—absolutely—about everything, and not trust myself at all.

If any man be in Christ, he is a new creature: old things are passed away; behold, all things are become new (2 Cor. 5:17).

15

A Saddle for a Horse

"I just can't understand women," a really beautiful Spirit-filled Christian friend said to me one day. Then he shared his frustration. Seems he had been trying to find a hunt saddle to buy for the horse of his teenage daughter. He had been looking for some time when he spotted an ad in the newspaper for a saddle that sounded exactly right. Planning to surprise his daughter with the saddle for her birthday, he telephoned the woman who had run the ad. After a brief conversation, he was satisfied that she had just the saddle he needed.

"How much do you want for it?" he asked.

"Well," she said, "I want two hundred dollars for it, but a boy who works with me here on the place has offered me a hundred and fifty—only he'll have to sell some of his things in order to get up the money to pay for it."

Thereupon, my friend made an appointment to see the saddle the following afternoon.

The next day, he drove the forty-odd miles to the town where the woman lived, examined the saddle, and found it met all his requirements.

"I'll give you one hundred sixty dollars for it," he said.

"One hundred sixty!" she sputtered. "I told you over the phone I wouldn't take less than two hundred for it!"

Having assumed from their previous conversation that

she would consider a lesser offer, our Spirit-filled friend was too exasperated to say anything, much. He thinks he turned away, mumbling something about, "If I'd known that, I wouldn't have driven all the way over here to look at the fool thing."

When he finished recounting his maladventure to me, my friend was still full of frustration and exasperation.

"I just can't understand women," he said again. He being far more mature in trusting the Lord than I was, I did not consider it seemly for me to express myself. But I thought someone should point out to him, "Look, fellow, this is exactly what Christianity is all about. The woman might have misled you, all right, but you weren't there to be disgusted with her imperfection, but to love her in spite of it, and to offer some kind of a witness to her—of good humor or forgiveness. Maybe even talk to her about Jesus. How will she ever know there is a way that belongs to the world and a way that belongs to those who follow the Lord if no one ever demonstrates the difference to her?"

Lord, you know how self-righteous I felt about how he should have shared the good news with her, to make a difference in her life. But, Lord, you know also how long it took for the truth to sink in to me that I should not have kept my silence either, but gently, lovingly, pointed out to him what his God-given role might have been in it, had he been properly sensitive to your leading.

Lord, for so many years, I interfered with other people too much, telling them what to do, what to say, where they ought to go. That was sin in me, I know. It was none of my business to instruct them in worldly affairs. But, Lord, let my former busybodiness in worldly things not act as a bar to our speaking the truth in love to one another, where the truth is made known to us, that we might grow together into your likeness.

42

Brethren, if a man be overtaken in a fault, ye which are spiritual, restore such a one in the spirit of meekness; considering thyself, lest thou also be tempted. Bear ye one another's burdens, and so fulfill the law of Christ (Gal. 6:1–2).

Rebuke a wise man, and he will love thee. Give instruction to a wise man, and he will be yet wiser: teach a just man, and he will increase in learning (Prov. 9:8–9).

Seascape

—the burnished sheen of sun glinting off the still water—

Lord, I never cease to marvel at the beauty you have made, so much I can't even take it all in through the windows of my senses, much less describe it to someone else or write it down to remember on a day when nothing beautiful assails my eyes. Thank you, Lord, for being so extravagant with beauty. Keep me tuned not to miss any of it.

And God saw every thing that he had made, and, behold, it was very good (Gen 1:31).

The Case of
the Borrowed Bicycle

'Guerite, our hard-of-hearing eight-year-old was home from the Central Institute for the Deaf in St. Louis, Missouri, for the Christmas holiday. We had all been enjoying her presence even though, admittedly, life had been less ruffled in her absence. We were all thrilled to see the progress she had made in her ability to understand what we said to her and even more thrilled to discover how her own spoken language had unfolded during the few months she had been away from home at her faraway school.

One morning our five-year-old Maria had ridden off to kindergarten on 'Guerite's bicycle, being accustomed to using it whenever she chose when 'Guerite was away from home. Later in the morning, when 'Guerite discovered her bicycle was missing and Maria's smaller one was parked in its usual place in the carport, she became quite upset, knowing that Maria had appropriated her property. There was quite a tirade before she calmed down and turned her interest to other things, and I thought she had forgotten all about it.

Not so, however, as I was soon to learn. At three o'clock, Maria burst into the kitchen door for her usual after-school rush to the bathroom, the fruit bowl, and my lap. She didn't make it to the first station that afternoon, however, before 'Guerite, with her hands on her hips, confronted her with vehement indignation:

"Maria, what you doing riding bike my?"

We all had to laugh, joyously, not at her anger, which quickly subsided now that the bike was on the premises and available to her, but at the fullness of the verbal expression of her displeasure. Only too recently the only sentences she spoke were mechanical, learned ones. Now she was inventing sentences, however imperfect, to express her needs and feelings. What progress that was! What good news.

God, it set me wondering, our joy at 'Guerite's imperfect expression of anger. Are there times when our expression of anger pleases you, when you can see that at last we are making progress, we are learning something?

If thy brother trespass against thee, rebuke him; and if he repent, forgive him (Luke 17:3).

Good Friday

It was the afternoon of Good Friday in April 1973, and I had occasion to drive about fifteen miles out into the country to pick up one of our sons from his work. I was alone in the car, traveling a peaceful unfamiliar country road, not the zooming superhighways where I had been accustomed to driving.

The afternoon was almost too beautiful to bear. I saw the farmers at work, their slow tractors purposefully turning the earth. And in a field, a live oak tree brooded protectively over a little white house. The earth was full of the glory of the Lord.

> Sun slanting down
>   on fresh-tilled earth
> piercing the clouds
>   Hallelujah!

O Lord, I thank you that all the earth glorifies you, that you have put yourself in everything you have made and that you have made everything beautiful in its time. I thank you for a frame of mind that lets even plain dirt turned over in a field fill my heart with rejoicing at your goodness. Lord, let it always be so, that I won't need to see some outlandish miracle, some fantastic healing won-

der in order to praise you. Let it be that I won't have to
see a hill to lift up my eyes to acknowledge that my help
comes from you. Lord, let me have that mind in me
which was in Jesus, to glorify my heavenly Father in
everything!

Let this mind be in you, which was also in Christ
Jesus (Phil. 2:5).

Irresistible

"Recommended for ages two to eight," the box said. Called "Airport," the toy had a baggage claim station that turned around and around to deliver the luggage checked through on the flight, a pilot who looked this way and that as the plane taxied for takeoff, a control tower fully manned with careful traffic directors, a top-of-the-terminal helicopter whose rotors whirred when you turned a little crank, and a diminutive baggage train. It was really precious. But I knew from their reaction to several similar toys in the past that our little girls wouldn't get much good out of "Airport" if Santa brought it down our chimney and put it under the Christmas tree for them. And so I passed it by.

A few days before Christmas, our college daughter and our junior-in-high-school one collaborated on a final shopping trip for the two little girls.

What did they bring home?

"Airport."

"I looked at that," I said, "but I didn't think the little kids would enjoy it."

"I don't think *they'll* like it either," my math-major straight-A college sophomore chortled, "but I just couldn't resist. It's so *cute!*"

That same holiday, another college student asked if she could take our kindergarten child to a petting zoo.

"My mother won't let me go by myself," she said. "She thinks I'm too old for that, but I just love those fuzzy little animals."

Lord, when I think of the joy that grown-ups have in things supposedly designed for the enjoyment of children, I can see a different dimension of the truth in "Except ye become as a little child, ye cannot enter the kingdom of heaven."

A little child will want to sit on your lap and look up into your face, Lord. And, Lord, I want to do that, too. Thank you that as you enable us to become as little children, we become candidates for heaven.

Let the little children come to me; do not stop them; for it is to such as these that the kingdom of God belongs. I tell you solemnly, anyone who does not welcome the kingdom of God like a little child will never enter it (Mark 10:14–15, JB).

20

To See What I'm Doing

Our five-year-old Maria was helping me clear the table after dinner the other day. When we had all the dishes loaded into the dishwasher, she asked if she could put the dishwasher detergent into the little cup.

"Sure," I told her and handed her the box with the spout carefully pulled out into pouring position.

She looked at it, and at me, and at the detergent cup in the pulled-down dishwasher door for a moment, then knelt on the floor, explaining, "I have to get down on my knees to see what I'm doing."

How I praise you, Lord, for revealing your truth to us over and over through the mouths of babes in every circumstance when we are tuned in to receive your truth. Surely what Maria spoke is true for us all—we have to get down on our knees to see what we're doing. We have to kneel before you if we don't want to be constantly spilling things and making a mess of our lives. Keep me reminded that before I do anything, I'd be wise to kneel —to see what I'm doing in the light of your word. In Jesus' name I ask it.

O come, let us worship and bow down: let us kneel before the Lord our maker. For he is our God; and we are the people of his pasture, and the sheep of his hand (Ps. 95:6–7).

21

Daylight Saving—
or Something

Somebody has decided that to conserve fuel in the midst of the energy crisis, we ought all to go on daylight saving time here in the dead of winter. The local school board didn't see that as very wise in our situation. It would mean that some bus children would be standing outside in the dark for school bus pick-up at 5:45 sun time, more than an hour before dawn. The solution proposed was to begin school later than usual, at 9:00 instead of 8:30, with the buses beginning their routes three-quarters of an hour later than the present schedule. School would be out correspondingly later in the afternoon.

It was recognized that the new hours would create hardships for many people who had their working schedules arranged to drop children off to school on the way to work, but the board made a special appeal to people not to leave their kids at school too early. After a couple of months, when earlier daylight made it feasible, the schools would revert to their former schedules.

O Lord, how complicated all our schemings to improve things invariably become. Everything is related to everything else, and the chain of complexity never gets finished until it gets back full circle, the problems always chasing themselves around and around.

Every solution of men creates new problems. I thank you, Lord, that it is not so with your solutions, that if we could trust you as the solution to every problem—and Lord, I know you are—we could stop meandering madly through the maze ourselves and walk in the clarity and simplicity of your light. Thank you, Lord, that you always make everything so simple by handling all the intricate complexities so efficiently all by yourself that it's as if the complexities didn't exist. And, Lord, keep on bringing me closer and closer to the point where I am willing to trust you in all things instead of trusting in my own ridiculously inadequate complicated contrivings.

For my thoughts are not your thoughts, neither are your ways my ways, saith the Lord. For as the heavens are higher than the earth, so are my ways higher than your ways, and my thoughts than your thoughts (Isa. 55:8–9).

A Free Ticket

There was a circus or county fair or jaycee carnival or something in town, and the kindergarten kids in public school were being encouraged to go by way of free tickets passed out. Maria was happy that she was going to go.

"Today is good for my ticket," she announced when she came home one afternoon.

"No, your ticket is good for today," I said, straightening out her language.

"Well," she said, shaking her head, "anyway, my ticket is lost."

Our grand pronouncements and our discussions about them are often about that flat, aren't they, Lord. We say what we're going to do, make the most grandiose plans, debate the pros and cons, maybe persuade someone to our way of thinking or accommodate our thinking to theirs, and then, all of a sudden, the whole deal falls through. It's off anyhow because we haven't thought to consult you at the beginning and the middle and the end and at every stage in-between.

Lord, I know that Maria could go to the fair anyhow— a lost ticket wasn't that significant. But for us to lose track of your will in some of our plans, Lord—we don't want to do that, ever. Keep us keeping track with you, please. Don't let us go anywhere you haven't given us a ticket to—for keeps.

Now listen to me, you who say, "Today or tomorrow we will travel to a certain city, where we will stay a year, and go into business and make a lot of money." You don't even know what your life tomorrow will be. You are like a thin fog, which appears for a moment and then disappears. What you should say is this, "If the Lord is willing, we will live and do this or that" (James 4:13–15, TEV).

A Lonely Room

Our teenage Susan was talking one day about the differences in the kids she baby-sits with. "It has something to do with the differences in their parents, I think," she mused. And she explained that the parents who do more interesting things always have messier houses. She wasn't trying to justify the messiness of her room, I know that. (It's been inordinately orderly, here lately).

It's interesting to think about. A neat-as-a-pin house can be an awfully sterile place to live. I remember the lonesomeness of a hotel room where I spent the night alone not long ago in a city far from home. My, but it was awful! Turning on the TV seemed to mock the lonesomeness. I couldn't get with it, somehow. I wasn't conscious of being deliberately messy, but my subconscious must have been deliberate about it because the first thing I knew, I had the room looking almost disheveled—shoes kicked off beside the chair, coat draped across the foot of the bed, odds and ends from my suitcase strewn about —as if I was trying to make it *look* like home, as if someone lived there, as if *I* wasn't as empty as I felt.

Lord, give me to pray for those who are lonely, not just on occasion, but all the time. How awful it must be not to have people automatically in your life, to have to call

someone up and ask them to come by. Lord, let the aware-
ness of my loneliness that night make me more sympa-
thetic to people who call me just to talk. I could always do
without it now, but maybe not forever. Let someone be
mindful of me and tolerant of my interference when that's
the only way I'll have anybody in my *life. Thank you,*
God, for the lonely people in my life.

And he cometh unto the disciples, and findeth them
asleep, and saith unto Peter, What, could ye not
watch with me one hour? (Matt. 26:40).

Verily I say unto you, Inasmuch as ye did it not to
one of the least of these, ye did it not to me
(Matt. 25:45).

Table Talk

I'd been chatting with the woman across the table from me at a banquet held by some civic or fraternal organization. Several others had joined in the conversation from time to time, and when I heard the woman say, "You have the most beautiful hands I've ever seen," I quite naturally smiled and was interested, looking to my right and left to see the hands she was talking about. I wondered whose they were. They couldn't have been mine, of course. My hands had always looked less than wonderful. Soft fingernails that always broke off before they could grow out. Squarish thumbnails that belonged on a man's hand. I didn't even own an emery board or a buffer or nail polish or anything like that. The half-moons were eclipsed by raggedly creeping cuticle. And there were minor scars from burns and blisters, a couple of little brown spots, signs of hands belonging to a past-forty person.

But the woman laughed at my looking around for the beautiful hands.

"I mean your hands, Irene," she said.

"Mine?" It couldn't be. How could she think my less-than-ordinary-looking hands beautiful?

Something came up—the speaker perhaps, being introduced and holding forth. And I never got to ask the woman what she meant or to explain to her that my hands

61

weren't beautiful. Since that day, I've understood, of course. She knew about our family, something about my life (not the bad things), and loving me, saw my hands as purposeful hands, fulfilling hands, that did, partly, what God created them to do. She saw them stirring soup, sorting laundry, changing a baby's diaper.

Recently, I have begun to see beauty in the same way.

The most beautiful woman I have seen lately is someone who would never reach the cover of a glamor magazine. She was sick, her hair stringy and dirty, uncombed, her beard a little heavy for a woman. There was nothing about her features that I'd have called beautiful once upon a time. But even in her sickness, she so glowed with the love of Jesus shining in her, that she was beautiful, as beautiful as any person I've ever seen.

Lord, thank you that I'm beginning to get a glimpse of what beauty is about, your beauty. The Scripture saying that when you come we'll be like you because we'll see you as you really are, surely has something to do with the beauty of that woman to me, because I wasn't really seeing her. I was seeing, through her, how wonderful your love is. Oh, I just praise you, Jesus, for getting yourself in us, letting us reflect your glory—in spite of ourselves.

Beloved, now are we the sons of God, and it doth not yet appear what we shall be: but we know that, when he shall appear, we shall be like him; for we shall see him as he is (1 John 3:2).

25

The Windows of Heaven

It was a gusty March Saturday afternoon. My husband and I had just arrived at the Raleigh-Durham airport en route to Albany, Georgia, for the weekend. He was to speak to a Full Gospel Business Men's Fellowship International meeting that night, and I was to hold forth at a Sunday morning Woman's Day service in a church. Standing before the Eastern airlines ticket counter, we looked at the posting board for the number of our departure gate.

Strange. There was our flight number, all right, and the board said "Atlanta" (we were to change planes there), but the posted time of departure was 12:08, not the 1:20 that I had read on our tickets. I took a closer look at what was typed on them. Oh! There was a 1:20, all right, but the little squiggles to the right of those numbers, the little figures I had taken to be P.M. were 8P instead. I had read the tickets wrong. They didn't say 1:20 P.M. but 12:08 P. We had missed our flight.

Once upon a time, such a thing would have upset me terribly. And once upon a time, my husband might have had some uncomplimentary inner condemnation of me about my inability to read simple numerals. But it wasn't once-upon-a-time with us that day. We had been singing songs of praise and reading the Bible aloud during the drive to the airport, and we were both walking in the Spirit.

So, instead of either of us being upset with me, we looked at one another expectantly, practicing "In everything give thanks, for this is the will of God concerning you."

Our "Well, thank you, Lord, what is the meaning of this?" was not an indignant questioning, but an expectant joyful wondering about what he had in store for us that day.

We have learned that God has a purpose in everything he permits to happen to us—including our errors—when we are trusting him. We knew his power, and we knew that if he wanted us to get to Albany in time for the meeting, he could arrange it. And if he didn't want us there, we certainly had no desire to be there.

We began to make some unanxious inquiries of various ticket agents who consulted their formidable, voluminous schedules and shook their heads. "We can get you to Atlanta, all right, by a roundabout route," they said, "but there's not a connecting flight to Albany until after your meeting is supposed to be over."

Still unanxious, we telephoned our friend in Albany who was to meet us there. No, he said, there wouldn't be time for us to rent a car in Atlanta and drive the rest of the way, but he did have a Baptist friend who owned a private plane. Maybe he could meet us in Atlanta and fly us down to Albany. After several more phone calls and several conferences with ticket agents, the details were worked out.

Knowing that God was still in charge of our day because we had asked him to be, we were sure that he had some special purpose in letting our plans be changed. As we waited for our new flight, we speculated about what that purpose might be. Was it that the flight on which we were originally scheduled was going to have trouble

and he was keeping us out of danger? Or was there someone on one of the new flights to whom we were to witness?
We didn't know his purpose yet, but we were listening
eagerly to hear it.

On the first leg of the flight, we sat by ourselves. In
the rush of the day, I hadn't had any breakfast or lunch,
and because of the turbulent weather, I knew it would
be advisable for me to have a stabilizer in my stomach.
The stewardess had nothing to offer me, but a teenage
girl gave me what was left from her snack tray on a previous flight. I accepted the sandwich gratefully and
thought, "Lord, is she the one?" and was careful to get
her name and address so I could send her a book when I
got home.

On the next leg of the flight, Allen sat beside a man
who was attractive, congenial, but obviously not Jesus-
centered, so he witnessed as he was led, and we both
wondered, "Lord, was *he* the reason?"

We still didn't know.

Arriving in Atlanta, hugging our pastor friend and
meeting our Baptist pilot, I looked at his little Beechcraft
four-seater and wondered if the four of us could really
get in it. Could it possibly get off the ground with us and
our luggage? I'd flown in the big jets, but this looked like
a regulation-size grasshopper!

Still, it was all in God's hands, and if he wanted us in
Albany, we would surely be there if we had to sprout
wings and take off on our own.

The grasshopper did get off the ground with an over-
powering sustained roar—a much ado about nothing, as
it seemed—that effectively rendered incomprehensible all
our attempts at conversation in flight. Finally, I was con-
tent to keep my questions to myself and just relax and
enjoy the ride.

As we flew south, the moon kept rising out the window
on my left, growing brighter and more shiny silver with

every inch it moved up in the sky. On my right, just beyond where my husband sat, I watched a glowing red-orange sun sink lower and lower toward the horizon. It was as if the sun and moon were on opposite ends of a slow-motion seesaw, one climbing ever so gradually up, the other sinking ever so gradually down.

As I watched the changing light and the fascinating panorama of earth so close below us, I became particularly aware of the multitude of scratches on the windows of the little plane. The windows looked like refugees from a thousand Kansas dust storms—with some wind-hurtled gravel blown in for good measure.

There were long scratches and short ones, deep ones and shallow ones, curved ones and straight ones, horizontal ones and vertical ones, and other scratches that went every helter-skelter direction imaginable, a jumbled maze of meaningless, messy scratches. A pity, I thought, and it didn't occur to me to praise God for the scratches. They were just messy, that's all, marring my view.

And then, suddenly, I saw it.

The sun reached the center of the scratches on the window, and when it did, all their meaninglessness and helter-skelterness disappeared. Every bit of it. The scratches were still there, but I could no longer see them going every which way. All that was visible of them, when the sun was in the center, was the portion that reflected the glory of the sun, the part that became a shining part of a series of concentric circles, framing its glow, lifting up its beauty. There was ring after ring of light, one within another, all magnifying the glowing glory of the sun.

O Lord, I thank you for this wonderful revelation, this glorious picture. Without your Son in the center, our lives have been flawed almost asunder by the scratches, the mistakes we've made, the sins we've committed, the missing-the-mark purposelessness that has been the ugly pattern of our days. O Lord, I thank you for the transformation that has come when by your grace we have been enabled to give your Son his rightful place as the center of our messed-up lives. And then, Lord, you made all our mistakes disappear except the part that glorifies you, the part that frames you with reflected praise for your forgiveness, your mercy, and your love.

O Lord, I thank you for coming into the center of our lives with such a glow that we can no longer even see or remember the parts that were bad, that failed to glorify you. Lord, I thank you for everything you have permitted to come into my life, everything you have delivered me from, the good and the bad—especially for misread plane tickets.

By your mercy, keep yourself as the living center of my life at every hour of every day that everyone may see the reflection of your glory, your forgiveness, your power, and your love. In Jesus' wonderful name. AMEN.

And PS, Lord. I thank you that the misread plane ticket didn't happen that I might do something for you, but that you might do something for me, that you might show me something I needed to know. I praise you, Lord, for the love that goes to such lengths to open to me the very windows of heaven.

For God so loved the world, that he gave his only begotten Son, that whosoever believeth in him should not perish, but have everlasting life (John 3:16).

26

Sufficient unto the Day

The egg man walked in with our weekly three dozen, and I remarked about the fantastically beautiful spring day.

"Yeah," he muttered, down at the mouth. "It's pretty all right—if only it doesn't go and get cold again and kill off all the blossoms on the fruit trees."

Oh, how we limit by our fears the joy you long to give us, Lord. Forgive us all, Lord, for the frequency with which we spoil a wonderful blessing by worrying about what will happen if things don't stay perfect. I've done it so often, without realizing how devastating my attitude was to beauty and to joy. Keep me from such a sin again. Let me enjoy blessings without conjuring up a worry about what I'll do when they're done. In Jesus' name.

"Do not be worried and upset," Jesus told them. "Believe in God, and believe also in me" (John 14:1, TEV).

Take therefore no thought for the morrow: for the morrow shall take thought for the things of itself (Matt. 6:34).

Shhh!

Because she is a born wiggleworm and seldom stops talking except to sleep, I thought four-year-old Maria needed a little coaching before attending her older sister's guitar recital with me. As we got ready to go, I explained, "Now, Maria, you'll have to sit very still and not talk—so that everybody can hear the beautiful music."

"Behave like you do in church," was how I summed it up.

"I know," she nodded gravely, her lively brown eyes somber for a change. "Like church. I won't wiggle, and I won't even whisper, and if I get hungry, I won't say nuthin'. I'll just wait till we get home."

Lord, I remember laughing at what Maria said, but I should have cried, shouldn't I? Church is supposed to be the place where our hungers are acknowledged and satisfied, above all we could ask or think. And as for sitting motionless in dead silence, with our hands folded in our laps, my Bible seems to say that we are to clap our hands, to shout with thanksgiving, to pray without ceasing, and to do all sorts of other "unchurchly things" in order to worship the Lord in a way that will be pleasing to him and bring honor and glory to his name.

Well, Lord, I can't thank you enough for giving us a new

*church where we are invited to express our thanksgiving,
to show forth our praise, where we are even encouraged
to clap our hands and shout, "Hallelujah!" Oh, I know it
may not be for everybody, but it's surely for me, and for
Maria, and we thank you, Lord.*

Now Peter and John went up together into the temple at the hour of prayer, being the ninth hour. And a certain man lame from his mother's womb was carried, whom they laid daily at the gate of the temple which is called Beautiful, to ask alms of them that entered into the temple; Who seeing Peter and John about to go into the temple asked an alms. And Peter, fastening his eyes upon him with John, said, Look on us. And he gave heed unto them, expecting to receive something of them. Then Peter said, Silver and gold have I none; but such as I have give I thee: In the name of Jesus Christ of Nazareth rise up and walk. And he took him by the right hand, and lifted him up: and immediately his feet and ankle bones received strength. And he leaping up stood, and walked, and entered with them into the temple, walking, and leaping, and praising God (Acts 3:1–8).

As We Forgive

With six active children and a more than full-time job of writing and editing on my desk, I needed some dependable household help once a week or so, to keep the fuzz out from under the beds, to scrub floors, and do occasional window-and-woodwork-washing chores. For several years I had worried along with Frances, a young woman who came once in a while to help. She was a good worker, and she was a precious person to me, but for every fulfilled promise to come on Friday, there would be a half-dozen times when she didn't show up. Since she had no telephone and seldom bothered to let me know when she wasn't coming, I usually wound up doing the couldn't-wait cleaning myself, neglecting something else. When my desk work was sufficiently urgent, I had to let the house go and maybe receive weekend guests into the midst of an obviously un-spic-and-span home.

Sometimes, though, I'd think I wasn't supposed to take such an easy way out and would take the time to go to see Frances to find out why she hadn't showed up. After all, I wasn't helping to teach her to be responsible if I just forgave her every time she disappointed me. I needed to encourage her to do better, to be more dependable.

And so I made innumerable trips to her end of town to find out what the trouble was. Sometimes it was that there was no one to keep her children, and I could remedy that by paying a neighbor to watch them for her; sometimes it was that she had overslept, and I would wake her up and wait in the car while she dressed; sometimes there was another excuse—she needed to go to the doctor, she needed to see her mother; often she would just shrug her shoulders as if she didn't know the reason herself, and she would promise to come the next day. But she seldom did.

Although I knew Frances was a "nominal Christian," there came a day in the spring when I was led to witness to her about Jesus. I learned that she wasn't at all sure of her salvation, and I shared a few Bible verses with her explaining that she could *know* she was saved. We prayed together in the car as I was taking her home, and I gave her a new Bible.

Rejoicing all the way home, knowing that Frances would surely be dependable now, that she would keep every promise, I told my husband what had happened. He was glad for my witnessing to her and praying with her but doubted if it would make any difference in her reliability.

And he was right. If anything, Frances became less dependable than before. But one day when she had promised to come to help me, she did telephone to say why she wouldn't be available for work that day or any day in the near future. It seems she had gotten many weeks behind in paying the rent and was afraid to tell her husband. He was about to find out, however, because the "rent man" had told her she would have to move. Unable to face her husband with this kind of news, she had decided to take her baby and go to South Carolina where she could stay with an aunt for a few weeks until her husband got over being mad with her. Then she would come home again.

There was some money in the bank that I had planned

to use to pay off an obligation that could wait a little longer, and so I offered to help Frances out of her predicament.

"Would you like for me to catch up the rent for you, Frances, so you could stay on in your house? And not have to run away? You could work it out this summer."

She came by later that day to pick up the three-figure check which I had made out to the rental agency.

Once more I was sure that Frances would be dependable. She would be grateful to me for getting her out of a tight spot. And she was dependable—for two whole days. Then no-show again, and I went back to see her, telling her I could understand how working to pay off a debt must be kind of uninteresting. I offered to pay her part of her earnings each day and let a lesser portion apply to the debt.

Frances came twice more after that and then stopped again. I went to see her a number of times in the next three months, coming away always with a promise that she would work for me on Monday, or Tuesday, or whatever, but she never came. Not once. Then, just before Labor Day, I *really* needed someone to help for a whole week, so I went to see Frances again.

"Please be honest with me," I said. "If you can't come to help me every day next week, just say so. I'll see if I can find someone else. I'll understand—it'll be all right, but I just need to know. I'd rather have you than anybody else." She assured me that she would come, and I believed her.

Well, she didn't show up bright and early Monday morning. Nor did she come on Tuesday. By Wednesday, I decided I'd have to visit her one more time to find out what the trouble was. That morning as I washed the dishes and cleaned up the kitchen, I prayed about the situation in a new way. Always before, I'd prayed for God to make her responsible. This time I said, "Lord, this baffles me. I've

75

felt I was supposed to teach Frances something, and I've tried hard, but I've failed utterly. I don't know what it's all about, but I believe you have a purpose in everything you permit to happen. What's your purpose in this? Are you trying to teach *me* something?"

I couldn't imagine what that might be.

Having prayed, I began to hum as I finished the necessary chores. Funny, I sounded like a broken record, humming the same phrase over and over. What was it? Oh, yes, it was from "Rock of Ages," the part that says, "Nothing in my hand I bring; simply to Thy Cross I cling." I started thinking about how enormous and hopeless a three-figure debt must seem to Frances—as massive as the burden of my sins if I were required to work out their expiation for myself. There would be no way. I'd give up and quit trying. Maybe that's how Frances felt about her debt to me.

Along with the over-and-over of the hymn phrase, I kept remembering the part of the Lord's prayer that says, "Forgive us our debts as we forgive our debtors," and suddenly I wasn't burdened with the problem of Frances any more. I saw clearly *that* he was trying to teach me and *what* he was trying to teach me, the sheer blessedness of forgiving a debtor completely, with no strings left hanging, no hoping she'd pay me back sometime.

When I got in the car to go see Frances, I took along a bag of outgrown clothing from our little girl for hers. Aware that I might not find Frances at home, I tucked a letter into the top of the bag for her.

> Dear Frances, You did owe me [and I named the amount], but you don't owe me anything any more. It has all been paid. I love you, Irene.

Frances was not at home, so I left the bag and the note with her next-door neighbor.

And I came home, set free.

I don't know if Frances's indebtedness to me—the money, the broken promises time after time—had been a burden to her or not. But being a creditor had surely been a burden to me, and I was glad to be rid of it, set free to just plain love, expecting nothing in return because the debt was forgiven. It no longer existed.

Lord, Frances didn't learn responsibility at my hand, but I don't find anyplace in the Bible where you say it is my duty to perfect her or anyone else. Instead, everywhere you tell me to love, to forgive, to follow you.

Lord, I thank you that whether or not Frances ever learns responsibility from anyone is not my concern. Perhaps she never will. Maybe she's here to be your instrument to give the rest of us someone to forgive; I don't know about that. And maybe when we have reached that perfection for which you designed us, Frances will be free to be perfect, too. Thank you, Lord, that you don't give up on us, that you keep on loving us, you keep on forgiving us forever.

And thank you, Lord, for sending me Rosa, wonderful dependable Rosa, as soon as forgiveness made my hands empty enough to receive her.

We confidently and joyfully look forward to actually becoming all that God has had in mind for us to be. We can rejoice, too, when we run into problems and trials for we know that they are good for us—they help us learn to be patient. And patience develops strength of character in us and helps us trust God more each time we use it until finally our hope and faith are strong and steady. Then, when that happens, we are able to hold our heads high no matter what happens and know that all is well, for we know how dearly God loves us, and we feel this warm love everywhere within us because God has given us the

Holy Spirit to fill our hearts with his love (Rom. 5:2–5, LB).

29

Adopted Kittens

"Guess what, mama!" Joy was bursting out all over the face of my fourteen-year-old daughter. I was glad to see it. The last few days had been rather hectically busy for her and her girl friend. They'd found four, tiny, eyes-not-opened-yet, abandoned kittens on a woodspath, mewing piteously in a drowning rain. No mother cat was in evidence; the kittens had to be rescued before they floated away. And so the girls brought them home and had been trying to keep up feedings with a tiny plastic bottle.

The results were not too good. The kittens seemed weaker every morning. Our own mother cat had kittens five weeks old, and Susan had tried to get her to adopt the new little brood, but the efforts were rewarded with hisses all around. Besides, the little ones seemed to have forgotten how to nurse. It had looked pretty bad.

But now, the "guess what!" sounded like good news.

"I can't guess what, Susan," I told her. "Is it some good news about the kittens?"

"Yep," she acknowledged, beaming. "The mother cat has adopted the new babies; she's loving them and licking them from head to tail, and they're sucking away on her like they'd been doing it all their lives."

"But how about her own kittens—the ones that aren't weaned yet?" I asked. "What about them?"

79

"They *are* weaned, mama, as of now," she proclaimed proudly.

I had to go see the transformation for myself.

Sure enough, the five-week-old kittens were happily sneezing into a pan of milk at the stable, while their mother was purringly nursing the formerly rain-drenched orphans in the kitty box beside the carport steps.

"What happened? How did you arrange it?"

Susan smiled sheepishly, waiting for me to guess.

"You mean—" I didn't quite know how to put it into words that wouldn't offend her, that wouldn't turn her off. I didn't dare say, "Did you pray?" I had to get at it obliquely somehow.

"Susan, you don't mean that you cheated—you didn't ask for the help of some—higher authority?"

The sheepish smile was still on her face.

"Oh, mama, you know what I did." She pretended impatience and pointed a single finger straight up, then turned and went about her business.

Susan had prayed, and he had answered—abundantly.

It was suddenly clear to me that a God who cared that much about stray kittens needing a mama would see to it that every lost person for whom we prayed would become intimately acquainted with his heavenly Father.

Lord, I thank you that nothing is beneath your notice. I thank you for your faithfulness to hear and to answer every prayer. I thank you for your loving kindness that is toward all your creatures.

Oh, give thanks to the Lord, for he is good; his lovingkindness continues forever. . . . He gives food to every living thing, for his lovingkindness continues forever. Oh, give thanks to the God of heaven, for his lovingkindness continues forever (Ps. 136:1, 25–26, LB).

30

Claiming Our Rights

"Smoking or nonsmoking?" the flight attendant asked when he was filling out my boarding pass.

"Nonsmoking," I said, and he wrote NS in bold blue letters on the ticket envelope.

When I boarded the plane, the hostess told me that I might sit anywhere in the second compartment. I walked back until I found a place for my child beside a window and a seat for me next to her. Later, after a young man had sat down beside me and begun puffing away, I saw the sign a few seats ahead of me. "Smoking prohibited in front of this sign."

I knew what I wanted. I was entitled to it. But I didn't get my heart's desire because I had failed to appropriate what I asked for. I had not paid enough attention to the signs, placed there so I could claim my privilege.

Lord, it's that way with prayer, too, isn't it? How often I ask, and how often you grant what I ask for, but I fail to appropriate it. I fail to receive it because I have been negligent about carrying through, claiming your promises, reading the signs in your Word about how and where and in what circumstances I might collect my privileges. Forgive my ignorance of your Word.

And, Lord, I confess there was another reason why I

had failed to sit where there was fresh air to breathe. I had by-passed two seats in that forward area because a young black woman was in the third seat. Honestly, I wasn't hesitant to sit beside her for my own sake, but I feared she might not appreciate our company. Father, how awful it is that fear of rebuff, or any kind of fear, has ever kept us from receiving the fulfillment of your promises, has ever kept us from sharing your love. Let it be that it will not be so with me again. Thank you, Lord.

Go in and possess the land (Deut. 1:8).

31

The Boston Tea Party

I didn't want to be impolite and talk while the eminent, intellectual discussion leader at the church was holding forth, but I did want to interpret what he was saying to the friend who had accompanied me. She had great wisdom but lacked formal education beyond grade school. I took a piece of paper from my pocketbook and scrawled an explanation for her.

"The Boston Tea Party he's talking about happened way back in the early history of the United States," I wrote. She nodded, took the pen from my hand, and wrote back a note of her own:

"But it don't concern Jesus." Then she handed the pen back to me. Her statement was accurate enough, but I defended the speaker. I have the rest of our written conversation still.

"Right. But this is a meeting about 'social action.' " That didn't settle it for Virginia. She wrote another note:

"The main thing is, the sun is going down and we need to know who Jesus is today."

There was more, but the truth had been covered, not by the learned speaker but by my unlearned friend.

Lord, I thank you and praise you that we don't have to be Ph.D.'s to know your truth. And forgive us, Lord,

*that our educated nonsense so often obscures the truth
that you died to save us, to make us free.*

I praise you, O Father, Lord of heaven and earth, for hiding these things from the intellectuals and worldly wise and for revealing them to those who are as trusting as little children (Luke 10:21, LB).

Let no man deceive himself. If any man among you seemeth to be wise in this world, let him become a fool, that he may be wise. For the wisdom of this world is foolishness with God (1 Cor. 3:18–19).

But all these things that I once thought very worthwhile—now I've thrown them all away so that I can put my trust and hope in Christ alone. Yes, everything else is worthless when compared with the priceless gain of knowing Christ Jesus my Lord. I have put aside all else, counting it worth less than nothing, in order that I can have Christ, and become one with him. . . . Now I have given up everything else —I have found it to be the only way to really know Christ and to experience the mighty power that brought him back to life again, and to find out what it means to suffer and to die with him, . . . I hope all of you who are mature Christians will see eye-to-eye with me on these things, and if you disagree on some point, I believe that God will make it plain to you—if you fully obey the truth you have (Phil 3:7– 10, 15–16, LB).

32

Church Newsletters

This week, I happened to receive newsletters from two churches. As I understand it, the church's mission is to spread the good news about Jesus and what he has done for us. It was interesting to me that one newsletter, a four-page one, had *no* Scripture, none of the written Word of God in it. The same newsletter had no mention of the good news, no mention of Jesus. It did mention God one time on one page. Among the words it did include were *horse opera, mechanized gunslinger, genuinely creepy,* and *Frankenstein monster.* Not much power there for combating the roaring lion who is out to gobble up Christians and non-Christians alike.

The other newsletter was only two pages, not four. Every page was saturated with *God, Jesus, the Bible, the Scriptures, the Word, the Lord, the Holy Spirit.* And there was a whole psalm reprinted in it besides, a psalm inviting God's people to praise God, to recognize his reality, to love his truth. There was power unto salvation in that newsletter. You could tell it came from a body of believers, a body with Jesus at its head. It seems to me that every church newsletter ought to talk about Jesus, the name above every name. He gave his *life* for us.

Lord, I know the solution is not to try to improve

church newsletters. That would be blasphemous. The so-lution is for us all to be so yielded to him that we can't keep from exuding him in every word we utter, in every breath we breathe, in every page we write.

O, Lord, I'm so thankful for your forgiveness, that you keep reminding us that we are in the world but not of the world, that we are of you. And that you will keep us. Thanks, Lord.

God . . . hath . . . given him a name which is above every name: That at the name of Jesus every knee should bow, . . . And that every tongue should confess that Jesus Christ is Lord (Phil. 2: 9–11).

33

Happy Easter

It served me right. It always does when I'm feeling smug and satisfied with myself and condemning of someone else's impatience.

On the Saturday before Easter, my husband had worked hard all day in the garden, plowing new rows, working in the just-right compost, and planting the seeds from packages with mouth-watering promises in pictures and descriptions of carrots and snapbeans and cabbages and tomatoes. When supper was ready, he came in and washed up just enough so that he could come to the table and eat without fallout landing on his plate.

Afterward, it was back to the garden again, to work at his labor of love until it was too dark to work longer. Then he came in, satisfied but weary, covered with dirt, ready to take an absolutely essential shower. While he was getting his things together in the downstairs bathroom, I went upstairs to start running water to wash the playground dust from our little girls and give them their Easter shampoos.

Seconds after I turned on the faucet labeled HOT, the realization struck me.

We were out of hot water.

Not a drop remained.

It was all stone cold.

Thinking about it, I could understand why. I had washed numerous loads of clothes that day, the dishwasher had gone through its cycles several times, and a couple of our long-haired teenagers had showered and shampooed. All put together, that was more than enough to have exhausted anybody's hot water supply.

Dreading to do it, I ran downstairs and tapped on the bathroom door. He hadn't turned the shower on yet.

"I'm sorry, daddy," I said. "The hot water is all gone. I'll heat some for you. It won't take long."

There was no sound on the other side of the door, but I could feel the vibrations of anger, and I knew he had heard me. Hurriedly, I turned on all four of the burners on the stove and filled our largest cooking containers with water and put them on to heat. Allen came out of the bathroom and walked over to the stove to look grimly into them.

"I'm sorry," I said again and told him what had used up the hot water. "I just wasn't thinking about everyone's wanting to bathe, or I wouldn't have run the dishwasher after supper and done that other load of clothes."

I don't remember exactly what he said, but there was no ring of "Praise the Lord" to it. None whatsoever. And the twitching of the muscle in his jaw was eloquent evidence of an ungodly frustration and exasperation.

I had some unexpressed thoughts of my own. Self-righteous ones, mostly. Oh, I was genuinely sorry about the no-hot-water. I was sympathetic. But did he have to be so condemning about it? So ugly inside? Hadn't we been learning to be thankful for everything and recommending to others that they give thanks for everything, too? Being thankful for good things didn't count. That was too easy. That came naturally. What mattered, what could make a difference in our lives, was being thankful, praising God, in the midst of bad things like no-hot-water when you were tired and filthy dirty. I was tempted to remind him of it, but the time was inopportune, I decided.

I don't remember what exactly, but there was some hereafter, some leftover repercussions of the water business on Easter morning at the breakfast table. And I was still self-righteous and above all that. The word *hypocrite* skated through my mind a time or two as I thought how he was making our glorious Easter get off to such a grim, glum beginning.

At least the weather was beautiful. And I got the turkey stuffed and in the oven soon enough that the eight of us got off for Sunday school on time.

After church, I took the turkey from the oven, made the gravy, and heated the vegetables I had prepared the day before. It was a good dinner. As soon as the two little girls had finished eating, I excused myself from the table and took them upstairs for their necessary naps, leaving the others to finish their eating and chatting. The little ones would go to sleep promptly if I stayed with them to see to "no nonsense." There'd be a no-nap free-for-all if I went downstairs before they were sound asleep.

While they were settling themselves peaceably under my eagle eye, I heard from downstairs the scraping of chairs being shoved away from the table and then the tinkling of silverware (stainless steel, if you want to be technical), a homey clattering of dishes, and an almost musical ringing of pots and pans as if someone was starting the work of cleaning up for me. That was nice. That was acceptable. But it would have been all right if they'd left it for me.

It didn't take long for the little ones' eyes to stop fluttering, for their breathing to become regular, and sleep to be genuine instead of just pretend. I tiptoed out of their bedroom and shut the door.

Sure enough, my husband was busy at the kitchen sink, doing dishes the way it suited him, giving each piece— waterglasses and all—a quick sudsing before he put it in

89

the dishwasher. I began taking the leftover food from the table and putting it in suitable containers for refrigeration, covering some with plastic wrap, packaging the turkey carcass snugly in aluminum foil. I warmed inside at having him help me. There was still a lot to be done, but it wouldn't take long with two of us working at it.

But then suddenly, somehow—I forget how it happened —he was gone, walking in the yard, or reading the newspaper, or stretched out on the couch for a nap, and I was left to finish the work myself.

And just as suddenly, my joy evaporated. The anger, the resentment, the ugliness that welled up inside of me made his distress the night before seem like angel music in comparison.

O Lord, when will I learn not to condemn? I'm tired of falling into traps of my own making. I praise you, Lord, that you have shown me the right way to live—in rejoicing, in forgiveness, in love. Make me live that way all the time. Deliver me from judging. Let me leave that to you. I ask it in Jesus' name.

You are so sure of the way to God that you could point it out to a blind man. You think of yourselves as beacon lights, directing men who are lost in darkness to God. You think that you can guide the simple and teach even children the affairs of God, for you really know his laws, which are full of all knowledge and truth. Yes, you teach others—then why don't you teach yourselves? . . . You are so proud of knowing God's laws, *but you dishonor him by breaking them.* No wonder the Scriptures say that the world speaks evil of God because of you (Rom. 2:19–21, 23, LB).

Timing

My friend was entertaining her mother-in-law during the spring holidays. One day, something was said, quite unintentionally, that hurt the older woman's feelings. For several days, she did almost nothing but cry. My friend wanted *so* to comfort her, but every time she headed down the hall to the guest room, intent upon speaking a soothing word, it seemed as if the Lord said to her, "Don't stop the hurt. Don't stop the hurt," and prevented her from going.

My friend understood that God was doing a work in her mother-in-law, and if she interfered, the work would be interrupted before it was completed. She was miserable herself, but obedient to the voice of the Lord, and finally, on the last night of the mother-in-law's visit, the time was right for a reconciliation. What a blessing they shared together, then, at the right time. My friend was full of rejoicing when I saw her afterward.

"The Lord did it exactly right," she said. "Now we have a better relationship than we have ever had before. When she left, she told me it was the very best visit she'd ever had anywhere."

Thank you, Lord, for letting my friend share her experience with me. You know how I am. I like to keep things all neatly tied up, smoothed over, no loose ends dangling. But you've given me to see that a garden would never produce a bountiful harvest if no one disturbed the soil to plant seeds. And I have to disarrange the furniture to scrub my kitchen floor properly. It's the same way when you are doing a work—we shouldn't be too quick to try to tidy up, to put relationships back in a position that looks right. Sometimes raw wounds need to lay open and bleed for the poison to get out. Sewn up too soon, they rupture and make a worse hurt before healing can set in.

O Lord, give me the grace to wait until you say, "Ready," before I try to be reconciled with the person who is estranged from me. Give me grace to wait until you've finished with what you're doing in both of us in the midst of it, that your name might truly be glorified. Thank you, Lord.

To every thing there is a season, and a time to every purpose under the heaven: . . . a time to break down, and a time to build up; A time to weep, and a time to laugh; a time to mourn, and a time to dance; . . . a time to embrace, and a time to refrain from embracing; . . . a time to keep silence, and a time to speak (Eccles. 3:1, 3–5, 7).

Let patience have her perfect work, that ye may be perfect and entire, wanting nothing (James 1:4).

Standards

When we say, "I'll never forgive myself"—and I've done it—we're saying. "Lord, my standards are higher than yours." We're being the epitome of self-righteousness—and I've been it. "Forgive us as we forgive" has to include even ourselves and accepting God's forgiveness.

Thanks, Lord.

And forgive us our debts, as we forgive our debtors. For if ye forgive men their trespasses, your heavenly Father will also forgive you: But if ye forgive not men their trespasses, neither will your Father forgive your trespasses (Matt. 6:12, 14, 15).

36

Security Regulations

"No Conversation Beyond This Point." No, the sign over the airport glass doors didn't say that. It said merely, "Only ticketed passengers allowed beyond this point." But it might as well have said, "No Talking," because the passengers-only waiting room was full of people—and dead silence. Some passengers-to-be traveling alone were absorbed in their newspapers, their fingernails, in desultory staring at walls or out windows, in not staring at their fellow passengers, or in rearranging the contents of their just-searched handbags. The passengers traveling with someone were a handful of husband/wife combinations who had long since run out of things to say to each other.

It was the first time I had flown since the stringent security regulations had gone into effect. The elaborate precautions against sabotage, skulduggery, hijacking were time-consuming, expensive, and absolutely futile, I thought. Any hijacker halfway clever would have his gun disguised as an innocuous electric razor, a portable radio, a tape recorder, or a camera. There were all sorts of camouflage available for his weaponry. And I had read of lethal letter bombs, undetected by the postman who handled the innocent-looking envelopes. Surely the scan-

95

ning machines would miss them, too. Security regulations couldn't insure security.

Lord, what is it all about? Are you saying to me in the midst of it that when we put security first, security by our own efforts, that we will be not only insecure, but without lives worth living? Lord, give me to opt for life —noisy, friendly, being-with-all-kinds-of-people life, with those who are going somewhere and those who only see us off. Let my only hope of security rest absolutely in your hands. Thank you, Lord, for showing me how absolutely pathetic, pitiful, fruitless, unavailing, and ridiculous all of man's efforts will always be. Thanks, God, for letting me depend on you.

In thee, O Lord, do I put my trust: . . . Deliver me in thy righteousness, and cause me to escape: incline thine ear unto me, and save me. Be thou my strong habitation, whereunto I may continually resort: thou hast given commandment to save me; for thou art my rock and my fortress. Deliver me, O my God, out of the hand of the wicked, out of the hand of the unrighteous and cruel man. For thou art my hope, O Lord God: thou art my trust from my youth. . . . I am as a wonder unto many; but thou art my strong refuge. Let my mouth be filled with thy praise and with thy honour all the day (Ps. 71:1–5, 7–8).

Growing Pains

It happened a long time ago. I had taken one of my beautiful daughters uptown on a shopping spree for some new clothes. I thought our trip had been successful and that she was pleased with all our purchases. But walking back to the car, she seemed unusually quiet. Then, out of the blue, her head turned away from me and toward the store window. She said, "Everybody in the seventh grade wears one."

"Everybody in the seventh grade wears one what?" I wanted to know.

"A bra," she answered, giving me a defiant, ferocious look.

Then, her eyes almost spilling over, she added, "It makes me feel kind of left out."

I had an awful impulse to laugh, but stifled it and told her that none of the females in my family had matured early and that a bra—before she needed one—would be an awful nuisance, that it would always be climbing up around her neck.

"You can be a little girl for a while longer," I said, thinking how nice that would be for her.

But she didn't agree. "Even Sally's going to get one in a little while," she sniffed.

Well, I was undone. I didn't know whether we should

go back to the store and buy a padded bra to make her happy, or not do it because I didn't want her to pretend to be bosomy when it wasn't even the time for it.

Lord, we human beings are funny creatures, aren't we? Some kids can't wait to grow up, and some parents want to keep them children as long as they can. Well, Lord, I'm just thankful that you have made us all. And I don't have to understand why you have made us the way you have, but just love you and praise you, and, Lord, I do, I do.

I will praise thee; for I am fearfully and wonderfully made; marvellous are thy works; and that my soul knoweth right well (Ps. 139:14).

Dividing Line

Where does our soul stop and our spirit begin? The question occurred to me one day as I read a manuscript that seemed to make no distinction between the two. I felt there was a decided difference, but I couldn't discern precisely where the boundary line, the crossing over, might be.

Lord, thank you that there are lots of things I don't need to know. Your Word is the only thing sharp enough to divide between soul and spirit. Give me such knowledge of your Word that I will know all that I need to know and trust you for all the rest. In Jesus' name.

For the word of God is quick, and powerful, and sharper than any twoedged sword, piercing even to the dividing asunder of soul and spirit, and of the joints and marrow, and is a discerner of the thoughts and intents of the heart (Heb. 4:12).

Communion

I had attended small Episcopal gatherings before where an abbreviated communion service was held, but this was the first time I had participated in the full-length sacrament in an Episcopal church with nothing condensed or left out. The words the bishop and rector spoke were beautiful almost beyond bearing. And the words the congregation intoned back at them—to Almighty God, really —were fraught with significance and meaning to me. The physical elements were different from those I was accustomed to—thin wafers, real wine, instead of our squarish chunks of bread and diluted juice—and they made it more real, somehow, more preciously representative of Christ's very own body and blood.

Afterward, I went with the other women to the parlor where the bishop was going to speak.

We hadn't all been seated, even, before the first cigarette was lit, and then another and then another stuck between lips that still tasted of the sacrifice of God's only begotten Son. Holy temples of the living God puffing the air thick blue with smoke, stinging my eyes and nose with the burnt sacrifices to self-indulgence.

The bishop began to talk about Jesus.

I sat and wept.

O Lord God, maker of heaven and earth, creator of all that is, giver of every good and perfect gift, how you must still weep over Jerusalem. How can you gather us under your holy wings of love, how can you cover us with yourself when we would not, when we are so adamantly insistent on going our own way, on trying to find satisfaction in all the things of the world when you are in the very midst of us?

O Lord, give us to see that you are enough, that you are all in all, and that we can never have you as long as we seek something else instead. Deliver us from every turning away, every indulgence of self that still slaps you and spits upon you, scoffing, "Tell us who did it." Lord, we know who did it. We did.

Father, forgive. And give us so to realize the cost of that forgiveness—your only begotten Son dying on the cross—that we will truly yearn to sin no more. As Jesus gave us first place in his life, don't let us put him a poor second in ours. Thank you that he can't fit there. In his name.

O taste and see that the Lord is good (Ps. 34:8).

Cat Fur

Maria had brought the new little kitten into the house, snuggling him up under her chin, practically purring herself with the delight of a new little animal to love.

"Why don't you pat him," she said, holding him out to me.

I put a rather disinterested hand on his head, just to please her.

"Don't you like how fuzzy he feels?" she asked yearningly.

"Yeah," I said, still with my mind on something else.

"I wish I was that fuzzy," she said.

Lord, I thank you for the rapt attention that little children pay to your creation, for how much they appreciate a kitten or a dog or a flower or a stream. What's the matter with me that I can ever cease to marvel at your handiwork, that I can take it all for granted some days? O Lord, keep alive in me the joy of discovery of the wonder of all that you have created. And let Maria stay like she is—forever.

Out of the mouth of babes and sucklings thou hast perfected praise (Matt. 21:16).

Ocean Walk

Last summer when we were at the ocean, I was walking along the shore by myself one night. How I loved the ocean! I had recently noticed the verse in Revelation 21:1: "And I saw a new heaven and a new earth: for the first heaven and the first earth were passed away; and there was no more sea," and I wondered about the *why* of no more ocean when I loved it so and I knew God loved me and had promised to give me the desires of my heart (Ps. 37:4). As I walked along, I was singing a song I'd never heard before, just asking the Lord about it. The words that came from my lips over and over again were, "Lord of lords, you love me—why no oceans?"

I didn't hear him answer at all just then, but I was confident that one day he would.

A few days after our return home, a package arrived from a friend. It contained, among other things, a little daily devotional guide. I let it fall open, planning to read the passage for whatever day appeared on the open pages. The heading that greeted my eyes was: Sin—Gone with the Sea. The Scripture was Micah 7:7–10, 18, 19. And verse 19 was printed in the booklet: "Thou wilt cast all their sins into the depths of the sea."

O Lord of lords, I thank you that you answered my

question, that in fact, my question contained the answer, and that you opened me to receive it. Thank you for showing me that it is because you love me *that there will be no seas, that your love and your forgiveness are so complete that you won't leave any ocean around, like a bucket of scrubwater, to remind me of how much I needed cleansing. When you have drowned all my sins in the depths of the sea, the sea with all the unholy sediment will disappear. Lord, I confess that when I forgive somebody, I'm generally careful to keep them reminded of it. God, I'm glad you're not like me. I praise you.*

The Lord is merciful and gracious, slow to anger, and plenteous in mercy. He will not always chide: neither will he keep his anger forever. He hath not dealt with us after our sins; nor rewarded us according to our iniquities. For as the heaven is high above the earth, so great is his mercy toward them that fear him. As far as the east is from the west, so far hath he removed our trangressions from us (Ps. 103:8–12).

Advertisement

It was a beautiful ad. The boy and girl looked so happy, vibrantly alive and full of joy. The scenery was out of this world. Their view from the grassy hillside must have been among the most majestic that God ever made. There were towering rock cliffs, stately pines, and a thundering cerulean sea. It made me want to be part of the picture. It looked like truth, reality, a heaven of blessedness.

But wait. According to the ad's caption, the cigarette in the young man's hand was the key to this magically wonderful world. Only there was something contradictory in ugly black letters in a startling white box at the bottom of the page:

> Warning: The Surgeon General Has
> Determined That Cigarette Smoking
> Is Dangerous To Your Health.

Oh. That's where the truth was then. Not in the beautiful picture. Not in the words trying to persuade me of something else. But in the ugly white space with black letters.

Remembering a young, vibrantly attractive young man who might have posed for such a picture once, cigarette, beautiful girl friend and all, I knew the picture was a lie.

Truth came later when the doctors subtracted a lung and dosed him with maximum cobalt. Not many months afterward, an undertaker put the beautiful young man in a box, lowered it into a hole, dumped earth upon it, and rolled the sod back in place.

O Lord, forgive. What makes us like that—that we relegate truth to small print at the bottom of the page of our lives, a mere parenthesis, and are surprised when it takes command? Why do we promote the lie—and entice others to the trap with us? What would happen if the cigarette ads displayed the truth of once-vibrant young men in caskets, their breathless black lungs exhibit A in a porcelain basin nearby? If the liquor ads showed, not the lie of a handsome man holding a highball, but the truth of a drunk lying in his vomit, his wretched wife in a welfare line, his ragged children hanging onto her coat?

O God, don't let me live a lie. Let truth be advertised by my every action. Let "Jesus is Lord" be the full-color message of my life. In Jesus' name I ask it. Please Lord.

Know the truth! (John 8:32).

Love

Maria had been home from school for several days running a high fever. We were still giving her antibiotics, aspirin around the clock, alcohol rubdowns when she needed them, and comforting every once in a while. At bedtime Wednesday, I tiptoed into her room to check on her, to make sure she was adequately covered up. How beautiful she looked, her black hair a cloud on the white pillow, her cheeks still extra rosy. I reached my hand down to feel of her forehead, to see how the fever was, and when I had satisfied myself that I didn't need to waken her for more aspirin just then, I let my hand slide gently down the side of her face, barely touching it, to cup the line of her jaw in my hand, my heart almost out of me for the love of my child.

Every mother has done the same thing a million times and felt as I felt at that moment.

And it was as if Jesus said to me, "O Irene, that love, that mother love that is too great for you to contain within yourself, that immense love, that total love—that love is but the faintest whisper of my love for you."

Wow, Lord, oh wow! Of course, I can't pretend to understand the depth of such love, not even a smidgen of it, but thanks, Lord. Thanks for loving me. Thanks that

109

I'm not even expected to be worthy, that no one can ever be.

> This is my commandment, That ye love one another, as I have loved you (John 15:12).

Tears of Promise

For a long time, I had been aware of tears when I prayed. They didn't just well up in my eyes and stay there; they streamed down my cheeks and puddled in my lap or on the floor. I noticed the tears especially when I prayed with someone who had a deep need. They were so inevitable that I got in the habit of carrying a handkerchief to mop up the overflow. I noticed the same tears sometimes when I was speaking before a group of people and trusting the Holy Spirit to provide the words.

I knew the tears were not ordinary tears because when *I* cry, my face gets all red and splotchy, my nose turns on like a faucet, and I look like an absolute disaster area. These tears were different. They were not tears of sadness, nor were they tears of joy. They were clearly something else. But what?

I had come to take them as a sign of the presence of the Holy Spirit in my prayer or message. I felt that I could be confident I was being God-led whenever I experienced all that water on my face. It was precious to me that he would give me such marvelous assurance that he was hearing my prayer, that I was speaking his will. I believed he would answer such prayers and bring fruit from the messages that had the anointing of holy tears.

But it wasn't enough for me to have my own opinion

about what the tears signified. Every truth can be confirmed in his written Word, and I wanted confirmation for this.

It happened late one night when it was much too hot for sleeping in our unair-conditioned house. The whirring of the attic fan seemed to intensify the heaviness of the air. I knew I would melt if I stayed in bed any longer. About half-past midnight, I tried the bathtub for a while. It didn't help. Then I tiptoed downstairs and sat down with my Bible. It seemed the perfect hour to seek confirmation in God's Word about the meaning of the tears.

Many times I have just let the Bible fall open of itself when I was seeking his Word about a particular thing in my life. I don't remember being disappointed, ever. But this time I began my search methodically, using a concordance.

I looked up every reference to tears; the first was in 2 Kings, the last in the Book of Revelation. None of them furnished what I was seeking. That was strange . . . I had been so sure. But my question remained.

I don't know what happened next. Did I consult other references to *water* in the concordance? Or did my Bible just "happen" to open at the right place? Suddenly I was turned to John 7, and the verses leaped off the page: "On the last day, the climax of the holidays, Jesus shouted to the crowds, 'If anyone is thirsty, let him come to me and drink. For the Scriptures declare that rivers of living water shall flow from the inmost being of anyone who believes in me.' (He was speaking of the Holy Spirit, who would be given to everyone believing in him)" (John 7:37–39, LB).

I had my confirmation. The tears were not ordinary human tears. They were rivers of living water, a sign that his Holy Spirit dwelt in me and I in him because he had given me to believe. The tears that were not from sadness, not from joy, were from my inmost being, from my heart, where I had invited him to live.

This reassurance that his power was indeed working through believers was reconfirmed for me a few days later as I was reading in Ezekiel about the stream flowing eastward from beneath the Temple. The Scripture promises that the river will "heal the salty waters and make them fresh and pure. . . . Wherever this water flows, everything will live. There will be a new crop every month —without fail! For they [the fruit trees growing along the river bank] are watered by the river flowing from the Temple" (Ezek. 47:8, 9, 12, LB).

And I saw that we are this temple, and he is the river, and there is nowhere the fruit is not seen—even in me, when I am an open channel for his flow.

O Lord, how incomprehensibly wonderful that you give us unmistakable signs of your indwelling. How I thank you, Lord, for "holy tears," for every manifestation of your presence, every confirmation in your word.

And, Lord, while we rejoice to have this treasure in earthen vessels, we yearn to take on more of the likeness of the treasure. Let every outpouring of holy tears wash more of our earthenness away. Let us be transparent, the treasure shining through.

> A new heart also will I give you, and a new spirit will I put within you: and I will take away the stony heart out of your flesh, and I will give you an heart of flesh. And I will put my spirit within you, and cause you to walk in my statutes, and ye shall keep my judgments, and do them. . . . and ye shall be my people, and I will be your God (Ezek. 36: 26–28).